MW01698491

The metamorphoses must be undone.
-C. Olson

I will cover minor and major human settlements equally... because I know
that human happiness never remains long in the same place.
-Herodotus

So the first thing that they see
That allows them the right to be
Why, they follow it
You know, it's called bad luck
-L. Reed

She caught the rumblin', I caught the fallin' down
She caught the rumblin', I caught the fallin' down
I never see her, I never turn around.
-F. Lewis

"*The Blue Blueprint* verifies itself at every turn...Dodds has struck his note, has built a totem of modern myth. This is pure-breed poetry. There are some striking moments in this book that will change your life. If I ever jump to my death, I will jump with a book of Dodds' poetry in my pocket--if only to get one more person to read it. This is important stuff."

—Peter Clime, *Reno News & Review*

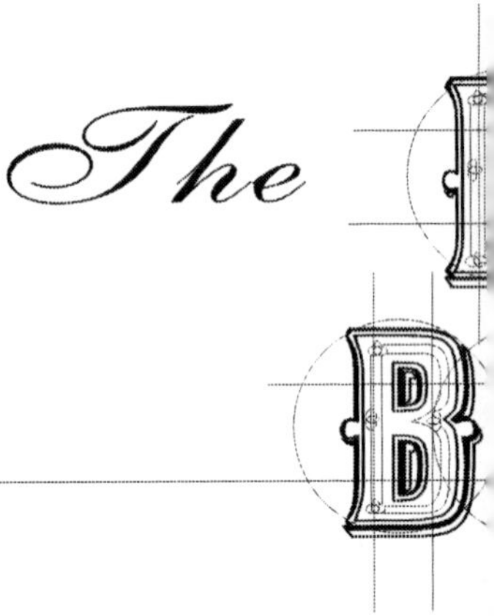

"The poems in this volume are beautiful, intense, and apotropaic. I can only advise to another, get a copy of *The Blue Blueprint* and give heed to its Word, or face the wrath of Dodds!"

—Aaron Seward, *Leafmeal*

BLUE BLUEPRINT

Colin Dodds

with illustrations by

Ben Gibson

(Struggle to Love, The Blue Blueprint)

&

Dan Jock

(Spill-O, Viscitudes & Songs)

CONTENTS

(Spill-O)

September, Afterward

MEDIUM RARE
PUBLISHING

A division of Medium Rare Industries
65 South Sixth Street
Brooklyn, New York 11211

This work is a work of fiction. Names, characters, places, and incidents either are the product of the author's imagination or are used ficticiously, and any resemblence to actual persons, living or dead, business establishments, events, or locales is entirely coincidental.

Book Design by Ben Gibson
Illustrations by Dan Jock and Ben Gibson

Visit our website at www.mediumrarepub.com

Library Congress Cataloging–in–Publication Data
ISBN 0-9721805-1-6
Printed in the United States of America
10 9 8 7 6 5 4 3 2 1

Spill-O

(Spill-O's Untellable Period)

Spill-O went to the unpopular part of nightmareville.

He made his camp far from entertainity,

in a half-comfortable place.

It was a tertiatory of his own, in the sunlight by the street,
among discarded rape mattresses, rubber fences,
in a field sown with splintered glass.

He played for the lowest stakes.
Breathing was nearly too ambitious.
Even the sun was dim for him.

It took a thousand monkeys
at a thousand keyboards a thousand years
to tell his story.

If a man had tried it,
Spill-O's name would have appeared too often
for it to be true.

But the period didn't outlast him.
The trick that got Spill-O through
was that he never looked into the camera.

(Spill-O's Sob Story)

Spill-O is charming after a few,
when he's fortunate enough to forget
the sky, the highway and most of the people,
all of whom he implicates
in his relentless decline.

"But no hard feelings,
it's not you and it's not you,
so hush,"
Spill-O says on the way down.

The angels all say he is doing fine.

Bald tires spin above their heads.

(Spill-O, Learning)

And in the end,
the mayor demanded
that the all astrologers get off the streets.

Spill-O punched his pillow.

He must learn to dream better,
he reprimanded himself.

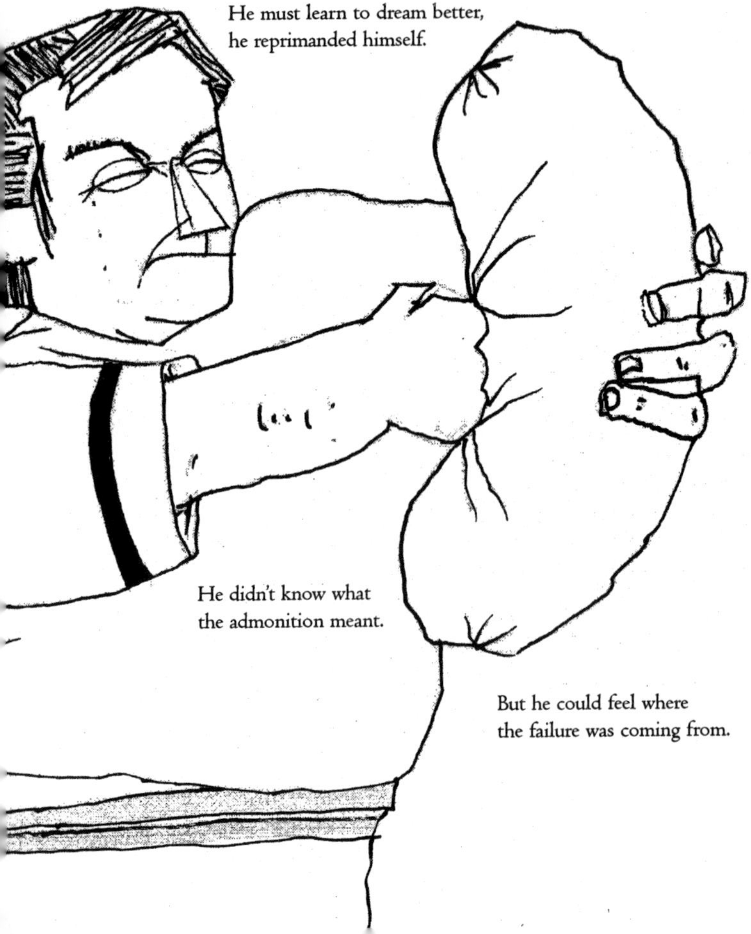

He didn't know what
the admonition meant.

But he could feel where
the failure was coming from.

(Spill-O's Crimes)

As a child, Spill-O desecrated baby showers and funerals across the countryside.

He slaughtered all his birthday presents in vast action-figure gotterdammerungs.

But alas, the blood on his hands was all his own.

Afterward, he never quite knew if he was in exile or on the lam.

(Spill-O's Easter, in Eight Parts)

Spill-O said he was only going out to see
the amazing things they're doing with failure nowadays.

But the hieroglyph strips in the newspaper
explain it better than that.

He was disheveled, weaving with the weeks,
but walked the stations of the cross all the same.

He was no pioneer in humility,
though a cathaholic.

He saw the roman standards
sprouting from penises in his sleep.

And he bent to see the women bent
out of their windows in the morning.

But, given the horrors of hubris,
his noblest sound had become a whine.

Thusly, Spill-O made his rough and humble
effort through mass.

(Part 2)

It was a funny night.
He began to get teary-eyed
over the fate of molecules
rather than the fate of himself.

At their last reunion,
Spill-O said to god,

"Listen, I'm through with trying to do it right.
I'm out of care and out of words.
This world's for shit, because of you or in spite.
And I'm going down to float with the turds.

"I resent the sainthood and the suicide.
You need to find a better way for me to be your friend.
Because I feel like I never should've tried.
Your favor suffocates and your grace gives me the bends.

"I'm going elsewhere, to a dumber shore,
to get too drunk to see.
I can't care to comprehend anymore
what you're doing to me."

God makes Spill-O see himself newly in the old season,
in the new year.

The father returns unrecognizable,
the son returns changed,
each wealthy or begging, and each strange.

As such, Spill-O,
with his fiery hair combed,
came to another easter.

(Part 3)

It had been christmas for four months
and nobody wanted to live anymore.
They'd tell you as much.

The townspeople advised Spill-O
to lay in the gutter and weep,
to let the municipal men
take him to where he'd be out of the way.

He was completely failurious in the face of victory.
He smelled of cigarettes and chicken soup.
Undisclosed sources
had told him big secrets in the deep meanwhile.

And the heart of life,
its lustful friction and unbearable contradiction,
was descending for its crescendo.

From the virgin birth
to the virgin death is four months.
Spill-O is never prepared for the rest of the year.

(PART 4)

The first bible teaches real sympathy
for the wretched, ever-cuckolded god
who is our creator and tormentor.

Like the alcoholic uncle
who has passed from drunken shame
to drunken absence,
nobody talks much about that old god.

Someone who is not the radio,
sings the national anthem
of the desperate moments alone with him:

And the father's cold stare,
the eggs bursting in air,
made it true, and quite right
that this was no nightmare.

And no one hears, this time or the last.
Spill-O hears it too often
and wishes he didn't.

They changed the name of money
and remade easter
as a bunny laying an egg,
a man giving up the floating tissue
on crossed popsicle sticks.

And no one heard
heaven's own teeth grinding.

(PART 5)

Consider god's answer to Job.

It is the response of a creature who acts entirely from inner necessity

to one who understands only effects.

It is the wisdom of undistracted solitude, and unmixed certainty.

In that god's unending drama,
even his children's most fervent prayers are rife with betrayal.
In his volatile mind,
the covenant and the heavenly city
are incessantly rewritten and invaded,
down to the last adulterous atom.

If only his own problems were more infinite,

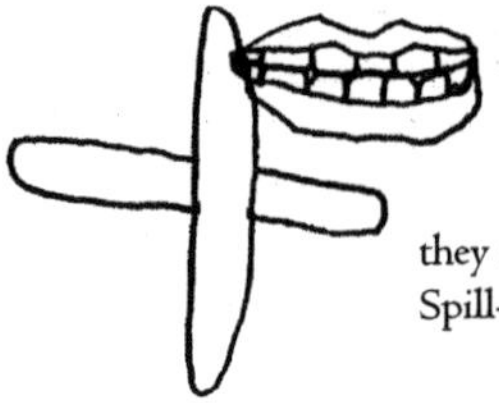

they might at least be reassuring,
Spill-O complained to himself.

(Part 6)

The bar was done up with easter eggs.
The neighborhood was covered
with pictures of bunnies and baby chicks.

Spill-O tried to identify himself and his yearly rebirth
with the whole world
rather than with the fate of one man.

Staring long at the cardboard eggs and bunnies
hanging from the bar ceiling,
he tried.

Spill-O wanted to keep the neighborhood's blather
closer to him than the passion and the humiliating horror
beneath its noise.

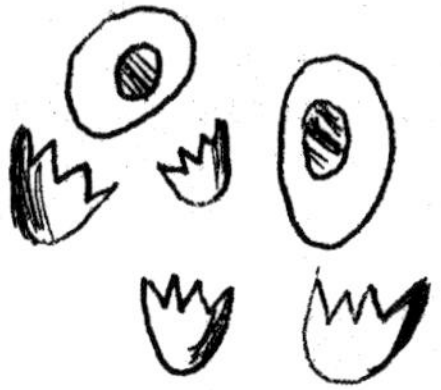

But the old season appeared in a new year.
And each rebirth is also a nudge forward

in a slow progress.

He remembers when the eggs were full of flowers.
Now, each is a funeral cake
with a bloody jesus jumping out.

And the sign in the bar bathroom reads

"Employees Must Wash Hands Before Condemning Christ."

(PART 7)

Subjecting winter moods
to springtime demands,
Spill-O walks past a little league tryout.

Fathers throw batting practice
at their sons' helmeted heads.
And the sons see faces like their own
on the baseballs.

His own father
loved to tell the story
of what happened to Marvin Gaye.

"Yes, every human atom cuckolds
every other atom
every reeking moment."

"Yes. I know."

That's about all Spill-O and yahweh
could say to each other
on some easters.

(PART 8)

Spill-O swears
he would tarnish heaven worse
than it has tarnished him
just to belong there.

And on the saturday night
before easter,
he does little
except swear.

He stays late in the illicit alley
where rhyme meets reason
and metaphor meets the world,
contemplating the adulterous atom.

And the adulterous atom contemplates him,
contemplates its own strong and weak bonds,
its many suitors, its many broken marriage beds,
contemplates its slow decay back to infancy.

In those sullied doorways,
god looks for trouble.
He marries the atoms into molecules
and whores the molecules into men.

And then on easter morning,
god makes real mischief,
pulling back the veil of decay, embarrassing
all the creatures he built to fail.

(Divine Complacency for Spill-O)

Spill-O is the animal who wasn't put down,
the eunuch who hid his genitals from the employer,
the rock-thrower whose house is already shattered.
Bourbon accepts what he has to offer.

From the casino to the ski lodge,
it's hard to string together the whole brutal story
of Spill-O on his weekend.

Chickens, cows, wheat and sky
were all killed and mutilated for the sake of it.
Old songs and silly fights and phony fires
followed wherever he went.

He escaped with the funeral ornaments
of better men in tow.
He hijacked the sun and shamed the shade.

The crowds around him consumed the time
apologizing under their breath
for eating and being in the world.
Each was waiting their turn
to demand that apology from someone else.

Spill-O defied them all.
At the very least, he drove a car.
He did it all because he needed a vision
that would forestall his surrender.

Old songs played on an old tape recorder.
The thunder rolled in.
But it was the kind of thunder
you could keep as a pet.

And his only vision was a rerun,
a vision of divine complacency,
of the god who can't be bothered
to do away with him.

(Spill-O's Garrulous Period)

It was in the young time,
when it was so hot that he sweated
out of the ends of his fingers,
so sad that he wept
out of the top of his head
and so arousing that he saw
out of the end of his penis.

A dream was his own, but Spill-O was alone.
There was work to be done.
He went down to the basement,
where his soul could not escape
and went on a year-ending march.

The dusk of the desk hovered above him.
A trail of paper and clothing
followed him wherever he went.
The only music that Spill-O could hear
was the crowd blinking in the trains.

But he never guessed the life of the mind
would require such a potent antidote.
The ambulance took him
home every night.

He struggled through the silence
in the soul of the surrounding conversation.
It was as though everyone was underwater,
but no one had spoken the word "water" yet.
And they threatened
that they never would.

Spill-O was the last ambivalent stop
in humanity's heels-to-haircut plunge
back into oblivion.
But he couldn't discern
whether the coming oblivion
was the blankness at the end of coitus
or the blankness at the end of thinking.

So he read the billboard signs.
The world was dumb.
And there was nothing he wanted more.

So he pulled the plug
on his monastic, searing silence.
He told everything.

That to him nothing was revealed
was the only thing
that Spill-O concealed.

(Spill-O's Obnoxious Tutelary Deity)

"I have to go take a piss. There's your myth."

The Monk leaned into what he was saying to Spill-O.
He carried water to the world on fire,
poured beer into glasses.

"This is the time
you get to know yourself.
But the unrest, even as you sleep alone,
will barely be bearable."
The Monk is polite. He clears his throat.
The storied truth knocks that way sometimes.

"Jesus only got a year and a month
of who he really was."
The Monk continued,
pouring more beer on the wound.

"Sometimes your heart is the lightbulb
in the solitary room.
Sometimes it is the crimson veil
that turns the late afternoon sun
to angry, hurried people."

The Monk talked with Spill-O all night
in front of the bar, and then inside again.

"You want to find out who you are?

Follow the money."

(Spill-O the Listener)

They called him Spill-O.
But what did that mean or matter?

"I am not what I thought I was,"
murmured through his skull.

Spill-O had fed himself past ripeness
on rock and roll's apocalyptic optimism.
He was madder than sisyphus with syphilis
that night, in and out of the bar with the Monk.

If he had been hit
by the truck he had such a romance with,
he knew he'd just
come out of another pussy.

"I never liked you anyway,"
resounded from heaven.

Homicide and suicide rates
competed in the center ring
of Spill-O's heart.
The scene was all dangerous.

It would have been
the best time of his life
if he hadn't been alive.

He was waiting
for what was happening to indicate him.
He was counting on a series
of familiar enlightenments.

"Take a minute.
If all you can do is be silent,
that's fine.
Just make an effort.
And try not to lie to me
this one minute,"
Spill-O pleaded
to his experience.

But being drunk all the time
works in mysterious ways.

(Spill-O in the Museum)

He cancels his appointments
and visits the museum ad nauseum,
to scrutinize the twisted striations
of christ's demise in a hundred carvings.

Why does Spill-O afflict himself
with such nightmares?
What impulse invokes them
on such a fine autumn day?

He wonders aloud
how he will resist or indulge
his own overwhelming sense of urgency.

And in his wondering
among the carvings,
he rules out no bad end.

He stays in the museum all day.
It is not a church, but a hospital for churches.
In its cacophony,
there is no real source of solace.

But solace pervades every painting and sculpture,
overruns their edges with a sexual glow
that no genital, not even the brain,
can drink from or understand.

Then, when solace yields to saturation,
Spill-O must choose whether
to be blinded or humiliated.

(Spill-O Deep in the Museum)

The hallways are full
of the famous ghosts
of other ages.

And there is a room,
where the hallways meet.

A woman walks its floor.
She is sad.
Spill-O will go to that room.

He will go again
to the virgin's unsullied lap
as a radiant child or as a broken man.

This time, he imagines,
he will not leave.

(Spill-O Leaves the Museum)

Spill-O asked why he was spared
the fate of the tortured.

"Because I like you,"
the curator explained.

As they left,
the museum burned behind them.

"What balls--to burn the museum,"
pondered the curator's nurse.

"And what a shame,
it had so many beautiful, ornate chairs,"

(Spill-O's Ascension)

The angel told Spill-O
about how the Original Boys
got so out of hand
that the Old Men at the Gate
had to rescind the big fun
and cancel everybody's raises.

Spill-O blushed to recall his peers,
who raped the backdoors to enlightenment
until every lit aperture,
even the stars, had swollen shut for good.

Later, after the ceremony,
Spill-O received a fly's-eye view
of his own conception
because he had behaved so well.

"Yes, you can go to heaven,
but not in this condition,"
he heard and then heard no more.

So Spill-O came back for another tour,
this time as a second-rate bodhisattva.

His words would have liberated
millions of beings.
But his mic was broken
and the drums were too loud.

(Senator Spill-O)

Senator Spill-O grabbed the dead hooker's ass,
kissed the nun. Nobody complained.

"I thought I could finger it out," complained the Senator.
"But the fact of the mater is that it's like quicksand."

He doesn't come down to the wharf mission
as much as he used to.
He's found another part of the rock
to rub his troublesome nerves on.

The maenads threw Senator Spill-O into the back of a van
and took him to the next party.

He lost his keys and his wallet.
They took his winebottle and he didn't care.
He staved off disaster with a taxicab.

He coiled a fate around the years,
but recoiled from that fate.
The year tied up into equal knots
and the days started getting shorter.

It was too cold for a toga.
And he woke with the meagerest designs on the day,
but was sucked out the door, nonetheless.

The taxicab didn't help in the long run.
Senator Spill-O turned grey and brown.
His camouflage fooled himself.

Walking his district, handing out candy,
he could feel the mortality
of everyone and of the dream that contained them.
It felt like snakes coiled around each breath.

And he could feel the gloom of the species
that's been in servitude to a hope
too large and distant to mention
since it could speak.

He hurried from the maenads' pancake breakfast
and over the marble floors.
His passion concealed the object
spinning at the center of his torment.

Senator Spill-O tended the only light.
Darkness danced into it always.

Madness pressed down through the air,
garbled everyone's hearing.
Chaos showed its strength,
strength like the weather.

But there was one golden shout
that demanded it be uttered
before the lights went out again.

The moon soared
over his unshaven, brazen form,
over the bank building and the gas building,
over Union Square,
just as he'd legislated.

That's why the backside
of the coin looks like it does.

(Spill-O in Hiding)

Love was as distant as the Byzantine age
and half as intelligible.
Still, every domesticated animal left standing
shoved it into Spill-O's face.

Holed up for the holiday,
He buried his eyes
in the tv and binged
on his grim mortal realities.

He ate when he wasn't full,
masturbated when the disgust passed
and stank deeply
underneath the stars.

The people on tv were either in love
or wanted nothing more than to fall in love.
They were killing themselves
just to get home.

Everything was broken, but somehow it all worked.
Spill-O laughed until mayonnaise came out of his nose
and cried until that got boring too.
No one heard and no one should have.

The tv invited him with pure white eyes
to the only emotional life, the only condition
for real abandon or real comfort,
deep inside the labors and levers of sexual love.

Spill-O turned down the sound on the tv
and went to a farther room with scraps of his youth
to try to piece together the story
so it worked without being broken.

(Spill-O's Passion, Explained)

With its impassioned tv voice,
with a thousand forms, faces, books,
the world stares Spill-O down.

All around him, room temperature souls
deploy their marketing armies
to vie for the loyalty of traitors
like himself.

The customers stare out
from their places in line,
carved in deep or shallow relief.

Spill-O saw himself
through the plastic windows on envelopes
and conceded that the demands were fair.
That was what was too much.

So he sought, so he fought
to think and be
like a statue, standing alone.

Spill-O looks for his soul
in all the staring, all the background.
And this time,
it's not hard to find.

It's the part that says
"I'm just crazy enough to do it."

(Spill-O Inc., Founding of)

Spill-O finally chased off his devil
and eliminated personal responsibility,
incorporating his habits and himself.

The company ran well.
Every good idea sped it up.
(But what was it?)

Spill-O Inc. trafficked
in the nouns profound
around the town.

It tried to ride the coattails
of the desire that won't retire
under welfare-colored skies.

Spill-O adopted the confidence
of the man from the future
who knows what will happen next.

"God willing, we will die soon,"
he said to his shareholders,
misreading his speech.

Employees worked together
and struggled against each other.
Spill-O Inc. had what Spill-O called
"the limited feeling of any success."

(Spill-O Inc., Insolvency of. Layoffs at)

But it was running out of money.
"I am running out of money,"
Spill-O said to his shareholders.

"All the doors threaten to open.
The landlord walks the streets tonight,"
he explained.
"I guess I give up on life too often
to adhere to a sensible financial plan."

It was spring and everyone lost their jobs.
Spill-O Inc. left them to wander
through unremarked-upon and unsanctioned afternoons
far from the vital, necessary center of life.

The layoffs were harsh
and liable to leave a man believing
almost anything about himself.

Spill-O, though,
was lucky to keep to his complaint
and his distraction.

And Spill-O Inc. kept living,
like many animals,
through its best efforts
and against its better judgment.

(Spill-O Inc., Eventual Success of)

Finally, the gray pages
fluttered and swooned
for Spill-O Inc.

The star-crossed company
had forced the alchemical wedding
of the Dairy King and the Burger Queen.

The money poured in faster than the days.
And sated, Spill-O went to bed after tv.

The rounded instruments of pleasure kept him in check.

He had charged the span and spanned the gap.
And there he was, a deflated balloon
He became ensconced in his own adequacy.
And we were all similarly trapped.

But now the King and Queen
are going to have a kid.
They say they'll call him Spill-O.

And that kid
will have to find a way
to live.

(Spill-O's Deathbed Confession)

Breathing his life out on the mattress,

alone and bare,

Spill-O failed to find a good thought anywhere.

All the thoughts had been made to order by men grown dull from fighting
for their quarter and calling it their half,
who made their names in freedom, kingdom and sex,
until there were no names left for Spill-O's epitaph.

But the whole thing took very long.
And no one came by, the way everyone does.
On his deathbed, in the last paragraph,
Spill-O says he knows he did something wrong,

but he can't remember what it was.

(Spill-O in the Car)

Spill-O says it's stolen.
He says other things.
Then he says nothing.

His story is so obvious
that if he looks beyond the next second,
it will all come spilling out.

September, Afterward

Towers Fell

We have been given a labyrinth,
a trauma so fine
it will take centuries to quite unwind.

Between us
and the thing that has happened
is all the feeble art
the weeks allowed us.

Towers fell.
But we did not leave the city.
We died but did not leave our bodies.
We understood.

Towers fell.
And, coming down, the babble became a pure shriek.
Papers, alphabets spewed out,
becoming nonsense and artifacts below.

Receipts, cashed checks, memos, schemes, instructions.
"The place was full of paper,"
says the tense man on the rescue bus to the center.
"And it all came out."

Creation Is Over

The thing that has happened
has turned Grief, Horror and Rage
into coins with blank faces in my pockets.
It is an old testament massacre.
Christ has been relegated
to nurse duties in the triage ward.

And my thoughts are no good.
They have the gist right,
but all the names are wrong.
Where towers stood,
a massive smudge loomed, a storm cloud
visiting a street address.

The spent change rattles in my pocket
and jingles in my headache.
A pillar of smoke sat on the earth.
A ladder of dust and debris
reached up to heaven,
and announced the new dispensation.

This will suffice for a beginning.
The curtain crashes farther open.
Creation is over and war has begun.
Dazed and lost faces fill the avenues
that told us to eat the flesh of the victim
and not be squeamish about it.

Something has happened
we couldn't swallow.
And no one on the street
will be happy again
until we've vomited up
this stomachful of murder.

Grief, Horror and Rage
crowd in too close,
too completely.
I am not wise enough to be wealthy
in this surging sea
of faceless coins and spent change.

God shouts too loud
for us to understand.
He spends the remainder of His day
playing with the leviathan.
We are as scared
as we are eager.

The Volunteers

We were there to will the apocalypse away.
We had failed, but still we stayed.

Our democracy and our fevered, austere hearts
had enlisted each of us as a part
in the body of that ancient priest who guides
the sun through noon and past the night.

In a daze, we did what we could,
though there was not much. We had cathedralfuls
of faith in our own sweat and elbow grease.
Our auxiliary gods were called guts.
The one above was an ornament by comparison.

We struggled in vain,
unable to weep
while the day waned.

We hadn't the imagination to have feared
the hole that now stared, the hole that now sneered.

Futility choked us and hopelessness
yelled in our ears. We ran to the salvation
army van for aspirin, water, whatever and anything.
Only, upon arriving, to say, no,
we were alright, and could we help.

The sun set far beyond the West Side Highway.
All the buildings wavered in the wind.
We waited to hear what anyone could say
while fire trucks and cranes rolled in.

And in this spring-field of the earth,
that struggles to keep its promise,
through the ruin, that promise shows its worth,
when the bookstores have sold out of Nostradamus.

You Don't Know What Happened

The old soldier briefing the amateurs
says you will be scared,
says you will be impotent
before the unflinching gaze of the dead.

Smoke and dust rise behind him,
hang around everyone,
reach all the way to Long Island,
where schools cancel recess.

Use scraps of cellophane
to stop up a sucking chest wound.
Use live electric wires
as a last resort for the dying.

Most importantly, he says,
if a body should wake
and ask what happened,
you must say you do not know.

"You do not know what happened.
You don't,"
he annunciates,
while another building falls behind him.

A Hundred Blocks Away

Returning to my lover, sunburned and dirty,
we hold each other
while fighter planes circle overhead.

We are a hundred blocks away
when we gently
undress one another.

Coins jingle
from my pockets
onto the floor.

In the grip of the last spasms
of the night, I call out,
my words no worse than my thoughts,

that life will win.
And I am convinced of large things
by small things.

Later, the sun rises over Queens.
And the smoke rises for another day
from the message too big for our minds to digest.

Invisible Helmets

War is not far.
That hidden, distant beast,
long banished from our conversations,
recovers his muscles. He is a stranger,
but makes friends fast.

The next morning,
we are all wearing invisible helmets
At first, they are only a headache,
a weight on the eyelids
and a valve on sight.

They will keep us from blinking
at the hell we cannot describe yet.
They will protect us awhile
from the folly
of questioning our experience.

Dead and Missing

The body count
is the news in the noise,
the diamond of the rough.

Each tally is every human story, start to finish,
compressed and told
with an economy of care, in a care-strapped land.

The mind that can only eat what's dead,
demands that the hot horror and uncertain story
be distilled into numbers.

The city, in its mild dementia,
revels in its respite from old desires.

But no one can listen too closely
to the new news,
even in these weeks when the newspaper
doubles as a diary.

Only the numbers, dead and missing,
make it through the storm of papers that still falls,
through the babble and the shriek that still resounds,
to reach us here.

Creation's Mutinous Devices

Now is the time
men ask themselves questions
in the daylight.

There is no time for idle eschatology.
Ruin has entered the room.
Airplanes, skyscrapers found work
in a war borrowed from the Bible.

And the land we'd claimed
in the elongated, impromptu
eighth day of creation
succumbed to its own mutinous devices.

The walls attacked the desks,
the phones attacked the airplanes,
the gasoline attacked it all.

The Water that covered
the face of the deep
rushed over all of it.

It washed over deeded land
as patternless rubble and intermittent fires.
Men and women vanished.
A world was undone.

And the Bible became
a lottery ticket
made illegible by the rain.

Lost in the Blood of the Lamb

Ghosts crowd the subways.
They are invisible light
and a film on the eyes.

All of it is lost
in the blood of the lamb.

The airliners take their pound of flesh.
We'd saved only ounces against such a calamity,
having frittered away so much at the carnival.

Taking the train home at dusk,
I cannot find myself in my clothes.

What is my alibi?
Am I the old soul who finds these things boring?
Am I the new soul who finds these things strange?

Disaster washes over everything,
unglues the facts from their attacks.
I am lost in the blood of the lamb.

In the Ruin

We are gone, so gone from that place
that we have stationed the angel
with the flaming sword before it,
just to be sure we could not go there anymore.

It's just down the street
from where the world hinges
on the difference between
one piece of paper and another.

Last week is so long ago
that the firemen digging through the rubble
have become archaeologists
digging in ruins.

They do so to learn how folks
lived a week ago, if any did.
They dare not recall a week ago,
but are lonely for it.

Fall creeps in like an anonymous letter
under a closed door.
Everyone is dead in the ruin.
But something must be done

to guard against our weakness
or find the right way to die,
to forget or subdue the knowledge
we summon too much of.

The will is strong. The senses
are subtle. The intelligence is deep.
This is not easy
and does not end.

It is the time after the cracked glass
has been shattered anew.
after we've been slaughtered, but before
we've undertaken a slaughter of our own.

By the deli, the jewelry store with its sale,
our neighbors rot in an uneven cage.
There is nothing beneath them but gold
and nothing above them but the sickened living.

The firemen do not dig for clues
The case is open and shut. Nor for the dead.
The dead and their world are so strange,
we think them odd stones shaped by chance.

Forgetfulness is what will wash us to newness.
We can not yet guess if a year, a life
will be the right length
for the forgetting that needs to be done.

The War Takes Shape

I was never much of a smoker,
but it was all so thick in the air.

The gods were aroused, desirous.
Their pheromones of fire and screaming
overtook our plans.

The stink below Canal Street
makes us mad for retribution.
The race of airplanes
unleashes its warrior caste.

Bloodlust is no weaker,
nor more complicated to arouse
than any other lust.

In the bars, the restaurants,
we talk war until we love each other.

Our conversations begin in diplomatic morass
and end in nuclear consummation,
tasting every permutation of horror in between.

And we hurry to the final explosion
just to be over with it, just to stop
wanting such things for a moment.

History and the old animal gods
squeeze us close.

We do all we can
to escape their embrace
and end up doing all that they ask.

The Subway Migrations

The subways traveled strange routes that week.
I wanted more than anything to be alone.
I spent a lot of time on those trains.
I saw everything through windows.

One night, on the train, there was a real skyfall
and everyone had to get somewhere fast.
No one wanted to die in transit.

That is the alpha and the omega of irony, now.
But it wasn't at the time.

Explosions and bomb warnings
took over the train car.
Newly minted colonels told us to duck
and made garbled promises on the intercom.

In a lull between explosions,
the trains derailed.
We passed the nadirs of our respective deaths.
And the great subway migration began.

We left the cities and floated over deserts,
past the suburbs of paradise and apocalypse,
our strange glaciers dislodging
empire and jungle as they went.

The conductors operate the constellations
like train signals.
Destinations ring over the intercom
like pledges of allegiance.

The trains go toward the sun, the cross,
the iron heart of irony, the mourning marketplace,
the falling sky, the train station of our dying hour,
but never stop.

On the migration, we are nowhere–
between one waystation and the next.
In the middle of the unknown story, we are no one-
between one name and the next.

It is confusing.
I learn the conductors' language
to ask questions.

Crossing over the great plains,
electricity fails for a stretch.
The train becomes a fugue of shadows
engulfed in a long mournful whisper.

In that hush,
the conductors finally respond:

"Ask all you want. And we'll tell you.
But you are little.
And no one listens to roadkill
wearing the footprint of the sky."

Ground Zero

The folding chair, the windowpane that survived
are what made ground zero so strange.
His blinking and his silent fires
are what made ground zero so like us.

Before he arrived, we were hunting out
the history of exactly what happened
to that child or this.
As if the milky way and the past that engulfs us
were just the wake of a gone locomotive.

Ground zero counts on his fingers
the ways god loves his children.
                                        Rainrainrainrainrain.

We had lived in a time and place
in which exactly nothing would explode.
Now everything ticks.

And I hurry off to Grand Central Station,
Grand Zero Station, Ground Zero Station.
I forget which.

The hours and the rooms lightened, untightened.
On television, where most of this happened,
ground zero went for a stroll,
showing his scabs and talking of rockets
in childish bad taste.

Dusk arrived like another catastrophe
that nobody had prepared for.
Women shook out their hair.
Men tried to be in the way.

Death had made a daring escape
from the nursing home and the hospital
and stared through our dream of everyday life.

It's cold now,
but everyone stands outside the store,
even ground zero,
reciting what they have learned.

Blinkblinkblinkblinkblink.

Christmas Eve, Afterward

Trying to find the reason in the bother,
Trying to unearth my future from his memories,
I spent the night talking with my father.

It was finally Christmas.
But the stores went out of business.
Neither side could honor the heavenly pact
Now that the city was no longer intact.

We talked women, work and war,
Respectful and suspicious of each other.
We talked about life before
And where a man could run for cover.

But our sense of the world had lost all its shape
Like a wire brassiere after a violent rape.

And we can't restart what's begun,
Or make our minds less like fists.
We reconcile ourselves to what's been done.
But we still withhold a kiss.

It's a funny way to be.
It's a funny way to start a century.

Everyone was out that night
By the church, the Christmas tree.
It resembled something right.
But we could do more than just see.

Finally, rain chased the tourists from the streets.
Leaving no one but the taxis and the cheats.

Vicissitudes and Songs

Great to be Here at the Hilton

It's great to be here at the hilton
I just hate sharing my room
with snoring saint john milton
and all them prophets of doom.

It has been days. I smell like everything.
Now they get me up here and expect me to sing.

You can't quite go. But you can't quite stay
That's the game we're going to play.
You can't get in. But you can't get out.
That's what our scene is all about.

Information can be obtained--
Another prison made of rain,
Another lover made of day-old pain.

And they don't give out wisdom anymore
Because wisdom always runs afoul.
Just give the asylum and the tribunal a tour.
It turns good minds to bad bowels.

But there's a puppetshow and a symphony
Behind your eyes, behind the bathroom door.
And there's nothing but a pile of money
Before your eyes. And nothing to use it for.

Tonight is High

A god is just a man who remembers who he is.
You remember you are in a strange city.
Love is not near. And you are an addict.

But love is not enough,
the law is not enough,
no family is enough
to tell you what to do.

Men invented jazz for the country
because improvisation, above all else,
was demanded of them.

The beer is yellow, the wine is red.
The band is praying
and you're out of your head.

It is the night
after a day of self reproach
in a strange city.

And you are no different
from the lucky victim of past ages.

Atop a pyramid, the Aztec priests
cut out his heart and held it up.
Otherwise, his heart would never be so high.

Tonight is high, you cannot resist it.
Simple circumstance and the sad story of the species
conspired to bring your heart here.

You're out in the open, the yonder,
free of the saurian bookkeeping
that stole the day.
Smells in the air hint at love.

You have learned one sort of thing
and are dying
to learn the other sort of thing.

All your dear apocalyptic hopes
have dulled with failure.
The sun rises and falls again
without interference.
You still long for the meteorological love
that breaks and drowns the ruling trauma
like midnight changes the day.

That longing leads you
through eyes that sort out cities
and cities that sort out eyes.

The speaking stops just long enough
to hear the band and take a new cue.

Failures of all genders yawn around you.
They say a prayer for christ and socrates
but say the rest to amuse
the town that kills those types.

Still, the saxophone leads your drunk ass
back to the pythagorean castle.

There's always been a short night of inspiration,
followed by millennia of degenerate generations
and cold, hard imitation,
when the tourists ask
if al capone and plato really had dinner at your table.

Those first nights are so fleeting,
you have to make ten thousand improvisations
to keep them near.

The Last Train From Grace

They tell you it's a compass.
But it's a roulette wheel.
They take you along to mass
But won't tell you what to steal.

It's the last train from grace
To the end of the line.
Take the people you can replace,
Try to tell them it'll come out fine.

You've seen my resume,
Read how I fell.
From the president's friend
To a realtor in hell.

Their voices aren't gentle,
When they finally call.
And none of them will help me,
If I won't be enthralled.

It's the last train from grace
To the end of the line.
I can't save any face
And I can't cover my behind.

On the train, where satellites can't see,
A moment of sadness is something very fancy.

But I can't give up the race,
I'm going down into the mine,
On the last train from grace
To the end of the line.

Hid in His Own Heart

I need a shot of cocaine to the pineal gland
and afternoon sex with arabian virgin princesses,
while majestic radioactive fireworks fire
from a platform on my back.

A big hole in my heart
drained the mystic healer's hands,
he said.

A woman wants to get closer.
She catches me and won't let go.
I want her to, then I don't.

The wrathful god also hid in his own h
He was laying an ambush. The goal is a
but the means are lies and kitchen kniv

I need real nudity, something bad for my cells,
bad for my molecules, bad for my atoms,
a superbowl assassination, a crown chakra extravaganza
that turns the desert to porcelain.

One day, we sin against each other.
One day, we become strangers.
We search the library desks and cash re
for new confessors.

Finally, our one need is to hear
from each other's lips one more time
that we have not truly been cast out
of the ever-troubling human condition.

I need something whose consequences overshoot
the trainstation at 4am,
when I am a zombie of pills and liquor,
on the platform where nothing gets remembered.

The wrathful god and I
had run out of grand designs and grand desires
with which to insulate our hearts.

He too abandoned his itinerary
of birthday parties and went farther a field
to think of what he'd done.

A Million Years on a Greyhound Bus

I've been on a greyhound bus
For a million years.
I can no longer speak for us.
But if anyone knows a cheer,

If anyone knows a prayer,
I'll be waiting everywhere.

I'm riding with people and their imitations.
We leak at every seam.
I'm sleepy, searching hard for intimations
That tonight is just a dream.

The streetlights and just one tree
Whirl outside the windows.
That's all that I can barely see
Besides the other, awful shows—

Like the bathroom parade,
And the ever-encroaching shade.

The party's over now.
Everyone's nursing their feelings
And rubbing their brows.

And the world is its own bastard child,
Nothing better and nothing worse.
No one knows if it's fierce or mild
Or if it's his or hers.

I feel like they hollowed me out
And filled me with broken toys.
I've been on this greyhound bus
Since the moment I had a choice.

My sorry mind is trying to hide,
Flashing dim pictures of the highwayside.
And if you ever care,
I'll be waiting everywhere.

Sans Euphemism

The story of my life
unfurled without euphemism
straight through the dull buzzing
of the alarm clock.

They tortured me
in the back of the restaurant
until four in the afternoon.

Then they expected me
to join them at a cocktail party
in the front at five.

The alarm clock blares
all day, ridiculing my faith
that there's a strategy
within this tragedy.

I have sat in the room of gentle chatter
and called my pain fathomless.
And I have never left that room.

I can pour a glass,
cook a plate of euphemism.
Not much more.

Thoroughbreds

For Everyone

We were all thoroughbreds coming out of the gate.
But some got up too early and others stayed out
too late.

We were all bright stars on a cloudy night.
Now the richest of us stone poor,
For having traveled so far from the light,
To boast that the jeweled trophy at the golden door

Was worth the bite and the bark
Now that it is getting dark.

And one by one, we were each crippled or belittled
in ways that stayed.
And the race just went to the ones who didn't
stumble coming out of the gate.

The Dinner Citadel

The boy I bullied when I was a boy
nods at me in the dinner citadel.

I have come here with the class of men
who understand that oblivion waits
in a misplaced decimal point.

Silverware sounds linger in the hall.
Steaks and rare fish crowd the plates.

The electric chandeliers above
do not exist for us.
The ersatz grandeur is only there
to take our money.

The man who broke the beige bank
strides to the podium.
Images of irrefutable success
flash across the screen behind him.

There is a strange horned animal
in the corner of his charts.
The lights are bright enough to hide his eyes.

Our unhealable wounds and unspeakable grudges
require we be in this assembly.

Meanwhile,
the crucifix on the kitchen door
tells the dining room the score.

A man washes my hands in the men's room
and says he can't wait for christmas.
I leave him a dollar and say nothing.
Bonhomie only makes things worse.

The audience keeps quiet
until the speaker shows his pride.
And, satisfied,
they hit him there.

But they do it subtly, the dinner citadel
was built on the presumption of limitless bonhomie.
It is our world, we share it while we must.

We surrendered before the war could start.
We learned our lesson without having to be taught.
Hands up, pants down,
we take our fate in sips.

And the speaker speaks the room out of existence,
dazzles us with his theory.
We are simple eating machines, he says.
Everyone, he stresses, has to eat.

Song For Danny and The Situation

Sorry to hear about your friend
But that's what friends will do
You take them around the bend
And they forget it's you.

I understand what you mean
But I won't give up the chase
You should've known you can't get clean
At someone else's place.

Each day teaches the lessons
Never handed down from above--
The strength of the delicatessen
And the failure of all human love.

We are deep in papers, in desperate hours,
When the screens hum and telephones wail
And the carpet soap makes the air sour
And the light panels make the air pale.

The days we pass in these clean rooms,
Are the bang and whimper of this doom.

Jaded money people. Water-headed shepherds of nothing.
Sex-tortured idiots with their hands in the till.
You-and-what-army wimps who don't know they're bluffing.
If the liquor doesn't get you, these people will.

We're heart attack guys,
lurching drunk at the prize.
Weight of the world dropped on our toes from three feet up.
Always searching, and only finding new ways to get beat up.

You only get one shot,
But it takes so long
To find out what you're not
And the ways that you went wrong.

Times Square Eliot

Walking in the rain
with a sickness coming on,
I am more mortal
than before.
The buildings go up so high
that it doesn't matter.

Autumn breaks through the dialogue,
the monologue.
The season asserts itself.
It starts about its business,
the business of all seasons,
returning.

Chaos winks through the car windows and the leaves.
Times Square Eliot is selling everything today.
His voice misses the crowd.
The crowd has its business decided--
counting up to five and back from five
and trading their bodies among the buses.

Maybe his words are obscure.
My situation and its aim
are no less obscure.
And the journalists' five questions
have not been answered by the five senses
nor on the five fingers.

My answers
have only grown more obscure
since they named me.
Every variety of uncertainty gushes through
the ancient tourniquet. And all we can do
is throw pennies into the pool below.

The Most Dangerous Thing to Be

After the war
We'll go to the stores
And tell the whores
Who fake their ahs and their oohs
To be friendlier about it
Because we used to be people too.

That's why we admire
Their forms over that of the fire,
Which is nearly as dear
Now that summer has retired.

There is no face, the world doesn't show it,
Not in the cars nor the trees.
You can be dead and not even know it.
That's the most dangerous thing to be.

The fog is thick, the dog is sick,
It's time to close the door.
The city always seemed like a ghost to me,
But this time I am sure.

The street is a failed hallucination,
A dream of wisdom that missed its mark,
A train that never left the station,
A lightbulb in the wrong kind of dark.

The air doesn't move, the wind doesn't blow it.
The light slants too funny to really see.
You can be dead and not even know it.
That's the most dangerous thing to be.

Times Square Eliot Elected Mayor

The headline spread
through the fevered fog of hieroglyphs
in the profane Central Nexus of town...

Times Square Eliot Elected Mayor

...out to the quiet profound streets of the suburbs,
where a new mayor doesn't matter at all.

I'm a partisan in the city,
my man lost.

"I'd like to thank the man who didn't murder me.
I'd like to blame the man who didn't murder me.
You know who you are,"
Times Square Eliot humbly annunciated,
as if he were taking possession
of the throne of the world, winking at me.

I should be quiet.
I should move to the suburbs.

Still, I linger, like a child in a toystore,
while the city roars around me.
It is a capital of transport, where no soul can stay,
where even the mausoleums are built like trainstations.

My man tried to say Times Square Eliot
was a failed seeker, turned away
at the threshold of the mystery
or that he was the seeker who'd succeeded,
and was waiting out the remainder as mayor,
without a care in the world for us.

But Times Square Eliot spoke too well,
with too much confusion, spit and sex,
for anyone to believe us.

He showed us and everyone
that we knew little of this place above its discomforts.
And that he knew them better than us.

Secret Drug Words

The secrets get told at midnight.
So I wait past the passing of the light
With eyes full of blear and blur
And a mind dull with fear and fur,

Because I think things could be alright
On another planet, on another night.

I woke up deaf after a year of dreaming.
I couldn't tell if the baby was yawning or screaming.
But the secret drug words that you said,
They still linger in my head.

The last time that I saw you,
You were trying to decide
Whether to be a five-year-old alcoholic
Or a hundred-year-old suicide.

I can't sit up and I can't stand down.
My birthday party don't make a sound.

Life Between Elections

The season of staring from a hillside
at the clouds' fabulous tits began again.
Nothing was accomplished. It was just
the time between elections, the days
between days. Trouble loomed.

It was the time I read too much to see,
when I lost all track of him and me.
When, in the nervous rustling of the boundless book,
I gave every strange sound a second look.

"And trouble is the rule.
Wisdom is only the scabstuff
over a wound too big to delineate,"
Times Square Eliot explained
in a radio interview.

He was struggling
to write an exercise program and biography
for the citizens.

"Station 4: Reach Nirvana. Come back as an honest person X10
Station 5: Reach up. Bend over and touch your toes X10"
The floor filled with crumpled paper.

And I doctored the quote.
I rocked the boat.
I knocked the mote
into my eye
and started to gloat.

Our reputations were capsized, then righted.
The calls increased, then began to taper.
Emerging from my own story, I was invited
  to visit his office of crumpled paper.

OLD MONASTERY TRICKS

Practicing old monastery tricks,
I waded neck deep into sleep.

The lightbulbs spewed rainbows
into the darkness.
The veil shimmied like a woman
and reached like a clean highway.

I was going for the one true god, the thought
like the rock that breaks the stained glass window,
like the amorphous lover I dissolve into.

I made nothing but wrong turns.
I went where the food wasn't.

Finally, I was naked
before the god who watches and asks,
just like mommy said it would end.
And the questions start.

My escape was much too narrow.
I'm hardly here anymore.
I returned to office work,
shot down the monday chute.

But nothing could make it better,
certainly not the daytime caffeine experiments,
with their pale lipstick hallucinations.

I'm no longer a fisher of the thing
that's as strange as reality.

Old monastery tricks
require a monastery.
Otherwise, you invite trouble.

It Is Noisy

It's friday night
at the trainstation/concerthall
at the end of the line.

And the performer's fools
are afoot, dressed like each other,
fawning over the sad fantasy of infinite vacation,
gurgling amidst the neon disclosures of the night.

The parasites from the crappy parts of town
infiltrate the fat, happy mob.
They are looking to con or strong-arm
the softies from the suburbs.

It is an irredeemable situation.
The only artist in the whole city
is a man on his roof who draws circles on the sky
with packs of pigeons.

Remaining here is a consequence.
But no one will say of what.

The city is a failed monastery.
The talkers show off their failed meditations.
The radios blare failed prayers.
It is noisy.

Talkin' Mo Mentum

You better get some things together
You better wait outside
Because I'm getting all balled up
And it's time to go for a ride.

Watch out baby, I'm coming over the hill.
If your daddy won't have me, your mommy will.
This man lives and that man dies.
I thought once and I won't think twice.

There's nowhere any relief.
I'm an engine that runs on grief.
But giving up on everything gets old.
Eventually a stirring takes hold.

I'm going to leave this awful town.
Yeah, I'm going away.
There's got to be a way around
The things that people say.

Two legs, two eyes,
If it looks like me,
Please say hi.

leave this town behind.
it anymore, don't want any part.
ful ache in my mind.
urnished room for a heart.

'm easily rejected and so full of rage--
ust the type to tear out my own page.
So look out mayor, I'm coming to town.
Don't shut me up and I won't put you down.

Horny for the Road

With a heart half-sick for eternity
and half-sick of eternity,
I borrow a car on a borrowed night.

I drive through the wooded streets
empty at midnight, by the baseball fields
and over the hills that once taught me awe.

The angel inside my heart has gone insane.
My woman has left me and I do not care.

The road,
because there is no other word for it,
is before me.
It is as near and elusive as a dream.

Eternity is still in play.
I need it so badly
that god could only be staring through the windshield.

And I am horny for the road before me.
I take all the pills that come my way.
I win fortunes from cigarette machines
and garden party craps games.

A car ride spells it out better
than the tarot cards and late night talks.
I feel the loneliness of the eunuch
and the yearning of spring flowers.

The stone in my stomach has dislodged.
I plunge down the empty streets,
half-trying to die.

My heart shows itself as a new creature
sprinting out of the darkness,
into the headlights.

Detective Song

Before his brain shut down,
He talked about hiding in my basement
Or getting out of town.

People are after him, is what he said.
They're after him, they want him dead.
He dreamt his neighbor's ghost impaled him.
He thinks someone put that dream in his head.

He remembered only one feeling:
Being a visitor, but not altogether welcome.
Uncertain whether to knock standing or kneeling,
He waited outside with the photo album.

I called it a day, called it a night,
Woke up where the river don't flow.
I stilled it, killed it and called it alright
And hoped the difference wouldn't show.

And after all my trying,
I'm convinced that he's not lying.
I hear the murmur and the rustling
Up there, the spirits hustling.

They're trying to get the latest news from the bugs
Because they can't live in the patterns in the rugs.

I may have been a bit too driven
To follow all the unseen leads.
I never meant to be in contempt of heaven,
But that's what the warrant reads.

Train Poem

Everything is slowing,
even the money comes too slowly
to change anything.
It is time to leave town.

The wind of the train
rushes like the blast of an A-bomb.
But it misses me again
and I get on the last car.

Opening a book, I read
what the old Roman tutor's best student
has to say about the heart
that does not change.

"The late sun is a determined demon
tearing through the trees and powerlines
from the vantage of the train,"
he says.

Of course, the nouns have been changed
to serve the bored.

The ancient mover is played by the train.
The many gods and their agendas
are played by trees and powerlines.
And the sun is you, reader.

The new life plays out on the inherited template.
We walk shoulder to shoulder with the dead,
through the ubiquitous iniquities of antiquity.

The book ends, the sun sets.
But the men on the train talk forever,
listing all the cities
they have walked around.

Great to be Here at the Ramada

It's great to be here at the ramada
I haven't gotten such an ovation
Since the players' lounge at masada,
When my songs were in heavy rotation.

This is the crossroads of the doomed,
Between solipsism and sentimentality.
I guess I'd always mistakenly assumed
That the love songs were only a formality.

In the greatest song ever, you make your escape
From all your worries, all the angels' red tape,
Leaving only one final crap in your pants
And a misunderstood word for the sake of romance.

Since that hill, I toured and lost my tail.
I trusted my stink that I'd prevail.
Now all that's left is to sing until
I'm over the line or under the hill.

The bottles we broke are broken,
The tall glasses are forsaken.
It all reeks of the greatest song ever
That plays at the end of a great endeavor.

Its message is no less obscure.
But we've handed over
Our hangovers
To servants to endure.

And if it takes away the pain
It will surely kill you.
But you won't let that detain
You, will you?

The Struggle to Love

Under Only the Night

She shuddered, jumped,
cried out unscripted.
She found a simple way
to make me shudder, to jump.

Her hands pressed
into my marshes, my streets, my towers,
my every house and dinner table
and into the quiet hair of everyone at the tables.

Her lips crept into
my every unanswered town and city,
every man in a quiet room reading,
every woman cradling laundry,
bending her body to another's eyes,
every boy shouting,
breaking windows.

She touched them all,
moving under only the night,
over my cars and forests like every wind,
every plague, every song
and every fear all at once,

But so gently
that it seemed like nothing at all,
only louder.

My Personal Undertow

You are my personal undertow.
You pull me toward the endless place
I long for and fear.

I am a swimmer.
You come to me
when my thrashing is through.

On the shore,
I pluck the sand from your face
speck by speck.

When we clutch and close our eyes,
we become an ocean,
a mute body giving itself to itself.

In the other ocean, you ask me
what that part of me is that reaches for you.
I say it is a fish.

The lights above the boardwalk
are the dream we meant.
And now we are dreaming it.

A wave, a ton of gentle water, a kiss
confirms the dream. Each takes us
nearer the center of oceans.

And your wine dark eyes
make a sea
of even my squalid apartment.

Picking My Nose

Picking my nose
next to a woman in bed.

She has been the side of nature
that cracks sidewalks with roots
and wrecks forests
with simultaneous fire and flood.

But she is sleeping now.
I am picking my nose

and she does not see.

The Book and the Act

She takes the dreaming away,
swallows crusty myth
with a moist kiss.

She takes off her panties
and says she doesn't
want to scare me yet.

The earth writhes against the heavens.
And after all the suspense,
the soul ejaculates at death.

She takes the dreaming away
because this is what
the dreaming always meant.

It is in the book as it is in the act.
(Chalk another one up
for sodom and tomorrah.)

Falling breathlessly away from each other,
we float, momentarily untethered
from both the book and the act.

Our limbs spread into cuneiform word-shapes,
we utter pure air and plain bewildered syllables.
The strangeness presided over by time evaporates.

And the sky becomes more than the sky.
And the soul becomes more than the soul,
and we become more than ourselves.

In the Dunes

We wander into the dunes
by the parkinglot and the breaking waves.
And we fall down. She travels,
eyes and ears, below my navel
to the site of the new story.

The sun starts its dive.
It is a spy plane, keeping track
of what always happened,
lovers walking hand in hand
to Jacob's vision of the tower.

The angels hold the world in place
with their will and desire,
circling up and down the tower.

They do not rest anywhere on it

visiting height and depth

to the delight of each, until

a connection flickers through the tower,

through the lonesome lovers, the lonesome angels,

fulfilling and ennobling all of it.

And she rises to my lips, to my ear.
And we whisper about our bodies
and the delight of their flawed union.

Sometimes flickering does count.

The sun has sunk.

The shadows have moved closer.

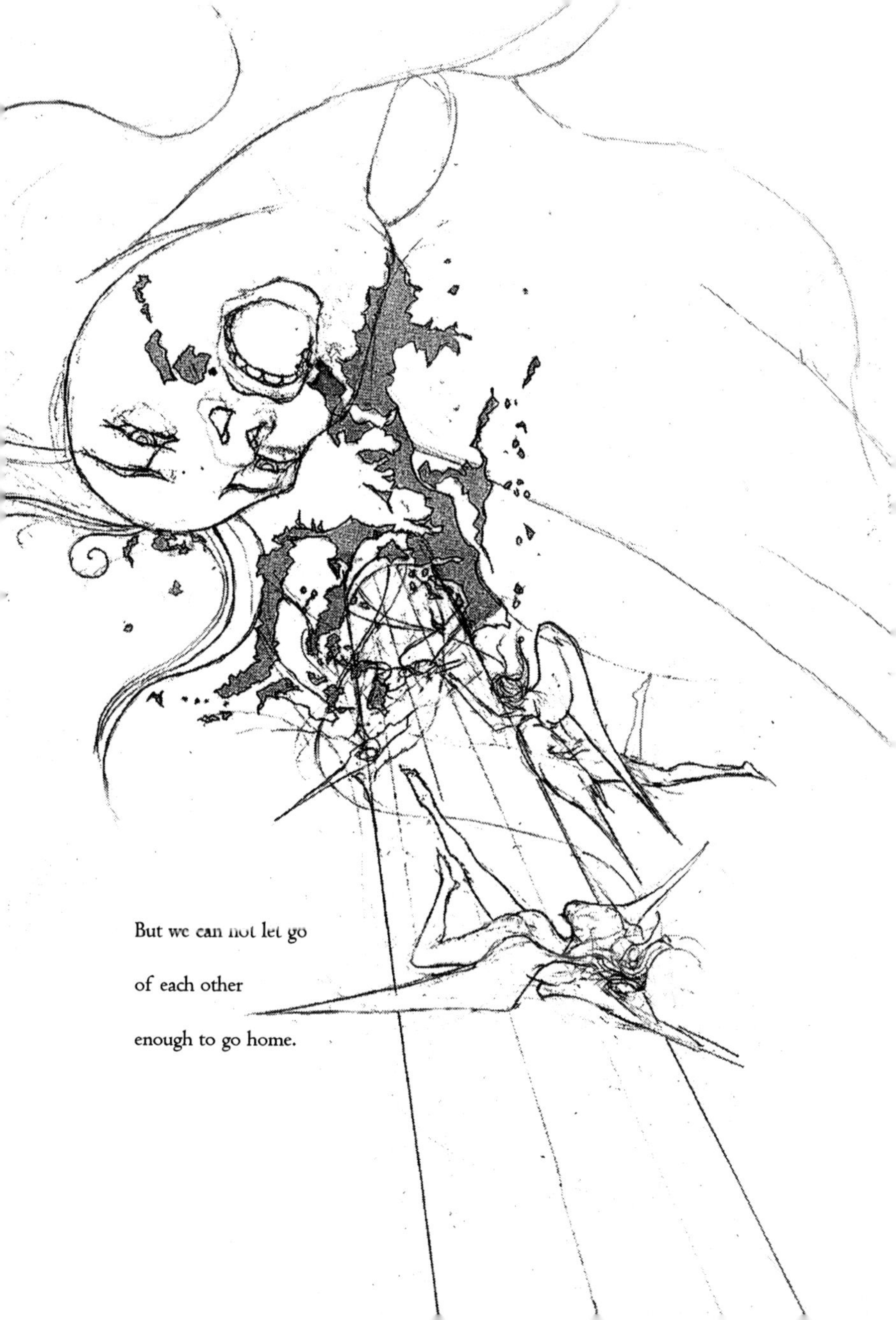

But we can not let go

of each other

enough to go home.

The Blossoming Frenzy

A.
In the motel, in her,
I blossomed.
And I blossomed again.

As if some unseen sun
were teasing me forward.
As if there were no thrusting
and no trick to it.

I have coaxed the world
to a frenzy with no wisdom.
I'll soon be torn to shreds.

In the lobby,
the sex of seeing makes me squint.
I can smell the light
and anticipate its lascivious come-ons.

I need to be among trees awhile,
among things that grow slowly
and die slowly.

B.
The municipal desk that escaped
the fire in the library
is in my office, if you'd like to come up.

In my off hours,
I coax the world to a frenzy with no wisdom,
repeatedly.

Aside from that, it's safe up there.
The light comes through the dirty lightbulb.
The sound comes through the edges of the door.

I remember the night of the fire,
some say I lit it, say I had motive.
It was bright, like sex with love,
light with heat, frenzy without wisdom.

It blossomed through the library,
sparing just a desk.
The witnesses were all silenced.
Memory itself forgot.

C.
After the fire, I was truly stranded,
alone with just lovemaking, handshaking
and other, more deserted habits.

I was blank, but jaded, knowing
I'd coaxed the world to a frenzy with no wisdom
and could only hide in my office
or await my tearing apart.

I can still fuck,
but not with my eyes closed.
I can still dream,
within limits.

A Question We Can Answer

We try like science--to the wall
then push the wall away. The bed breaks.
The floor splinters. We kick it to dust.
We throw each other away. And it never stops.

Finally we come triumphant, horns blare,
taxis and trumpets, inside and out.

We try until we are worn away
like stones on the edge of the sea
or carpet by a doorway.
But sex remains opaque and too big,
like gravity, to see from outside of itself.

Its riddle engulfs us,
turns from a question to a command.
It forces ambiguities between us
for our bodies to solve.

We do not speak.
Our language is too unwieldly
in the forest of our bodies.

We must kiss to make it
through the minute here.
It is a makeshift paradise.
Grace is fleet of foot.

We have found a question we can answer,
a telephone that works.
It is our ancestry and our legacy
to be close like this.

Of course,
there's a reason and a need.
But there is a lot of fat
on the sinews of necessity.

A Clitoris, a Sphinx

A clitoris, a sphinx
waits at the entrance to the mystery
that offers and teases,
promises and threatens
to swallow you whole.

A cluster of nerves waits
in a windswept land, an automatic body,
so experience could identify itself.
It has been alone forever, fantasizing conversations
with the wind, and has so many questions.

A memory discovers itself between her legs.
Light becomes a cloud of innuendo down there.
The memory and its chorus of rumors
may lead you out of the labyrinth
or it may lead you in.

A clitoris, a sphinx
waits with a bouquet of questions.
"Are you a perfect animal yet?
Can you subsist on spirit alone?
On meat alone?"

It stands forth, hides,
is irritated or pleasured
by the skill and whim of a man
whose guilt or innocence
is irrelevant.

The thread on the labyrinth floor
escapes the labyrinth to find love,
to flee love, or for rarer reasons.
It becomes a highway across a vast torso.
I ride it to a culmination,

a sphinx standing before an old city,
where the thread becomes a labyrinth
of streets and interiors
and the planet's memory
overtakes the planet again.

Every shape in the city,
in its marketplaces and its temples,
is a broken circle. The season returns,
but we are in love, we are at war.
We don't recognize those shapes anymore.

And Pythagoras smokes cigarettes
in the Port Authority and doesn't have
anything to say this time around.
He sells earrings and keychains
spread out on a blanket.

The broken circle, the human failure reminds us
how we must escape the labyrinth.
But the streets gossip like a nervous system
from the seasplashed fingertips, across the rural
inanity of the belly, back to a clitoris, a sphinx.

Eventually, every street is only one street.
She and I live on that street.
We climb into a room that's both secret
to the street and suffused with it
and make love.

The mystery buries itself deeper
in the labyrinth after each encounter.
It is an instinct of old things, of mysteries.
That's why we must be simple as empty streets,
when we meet in the dark.

A Telescope Among the Ferns

Our problem
is that we may or may not
be different
from the other animals.

In the observatory, we mock sex
almost as well as it mocks us.
It is repulsive through the telescope.
But it is the only thing
that moves me through the halls.

What reaches me through the lens
is not spring, but the collective grimace
of a species that has been awfully
and enormously tricked.

But in our vigil in the observatory,
the common fate of ferns both threatens and beckons.

Within our vigil, a suspicion lingers
that our dispensation
is only the patience the crowd has
for the heckler at the orgy.

Our vigil won't outlive life.
Every weekend, on furlough,
the sweet-smelling sirens of the valley
color my face with the markings of a clown.

And as for the other animals,
yes, we won.
But only we can say so.
How lonely.

The Pain of Impotence

He was busy,
in the massage parlor,
inheriting hitler's dysfunction--
silently destroying the world
because there's something wrong
with every pretty girl.

All his relationships with mommy, daddy,
the chair, the sky and himself
had only grown more familiar.
He was closer to crying than coming
when the woman enveloped him.
And the food had to be delicious just to be eaten.

The woman he failed to fuck later found him
and called him Cactus Doolittle in front of everyone.
He curled into a fetal ball,
bit his own tail and cried eureka.
But the world interrupted.
It asked for this dance and every one after.

And his manners only allowed him to accept.
But the world wouldn't let him touch its tits.
And the dance was a rhythmless lurch
with human partners only half the time.
The impotent man moved to a back table
in the dance club below Hotel Antarctica.

The patrons around him
commend themselves for their bloody appetites,
then commend themselves
for having sated those appetites.
Steeped in indulgence and starved of pleasure,
every comfort has failed the impotent man.

He can't escape. There's no place where he won't
have to eat to participate in the world.
He curls again into a ball and bites his tail
like an alchemical symbol of infinite.
But to the modern folks in the club,
he only looks like a sad snake.

The Ghost Is Loose

The day grips me in its blind careen.
But the ghost is loose, his suit undone,
straps drag on the ground, the pants are about to go.

I'm deep in the sanctuary,
pumping all my silver into the payphone.
I have the same old thing to say
but I don't want to go home.

A big suicidal thought
is afoot in the body, nudging the organs,
threatening to lurch at the truth
that doesn't compromise.

The only recourse left for me
is to hang onto the horn of the altar
and tug the day away.

I stay here all day, investigating a black hole.
They can take whatever they want,
so long as they don't take my mouth away.

I hold tight to the site
of every sacrifice.
The seed has eaten through the seed pod.
The ghost is loose, unsettled as the dust.

The empire was makeshift,
a stand-in for something else.
Intimations of that thing flash for no purpose
and give no purchase.

The judge's secret reasons for clemency
also flash,
but modesty won't permit my explaining.
He tells me a story
I don't dare believe nor forget.

I am leaving the grip of the day,
its specious and precious routine,
leaving the grip of the body,
whose desires are the only unequivocal clues.

The big suicidal thought rustles trees
and shatters into whispers.
I have lost a whole season
to my bestial habits.

There is a woman behind the map
acting out the most modern forms of relief.
In that pornography, every eye knows my story.
She and I do what we can
to speed the passage of the storm.

My failures and habits,
which once fit me so snug,
now dangle or choke me.

Clearly, the ghost is coming loose.

The Center of Sex

Everyone is a lover forever
at the center of sex.

Even the grass and trees
find a way to fuck you there.
Car doors slam.
It is not the knocking on the door.

The client races of dogs and cows
share your prison cell
and decorate it with semen-crusted hearts.
Flies flock toward the center of sex.
Churches made of cluster bombs
line its streets.

Its necessity pulls out your bones
and leaves only the soft parts
available for the demands
of the dark and gentle vaginal folds
that comprise heaven and madness.
All you can do is order pornography
and avoid the knocking at the door.

The flies finally reconstruct you
from your waste, your words.
You are reborn dirty, and can't remember why
you ever bothered with such an awful adventure.

The world radiates in all directions from the center,
from the mouth of the mouth,
from nipples within nipples,
tapping like blind men, screaming like infants,
it remembers you and returns, knocking on the door.

You hunt out the oracle with claws.
Only a creature that has been mutilated by the divine
can explain your situation.

And she just turns up her television
and goes into the kitchen.

But it is not the knocking on the door, yet.
Huge bodies are moving in your bed.
They will surely crush you
in a very small, impersonal misunderstanding,
then resurrect you to do it again.

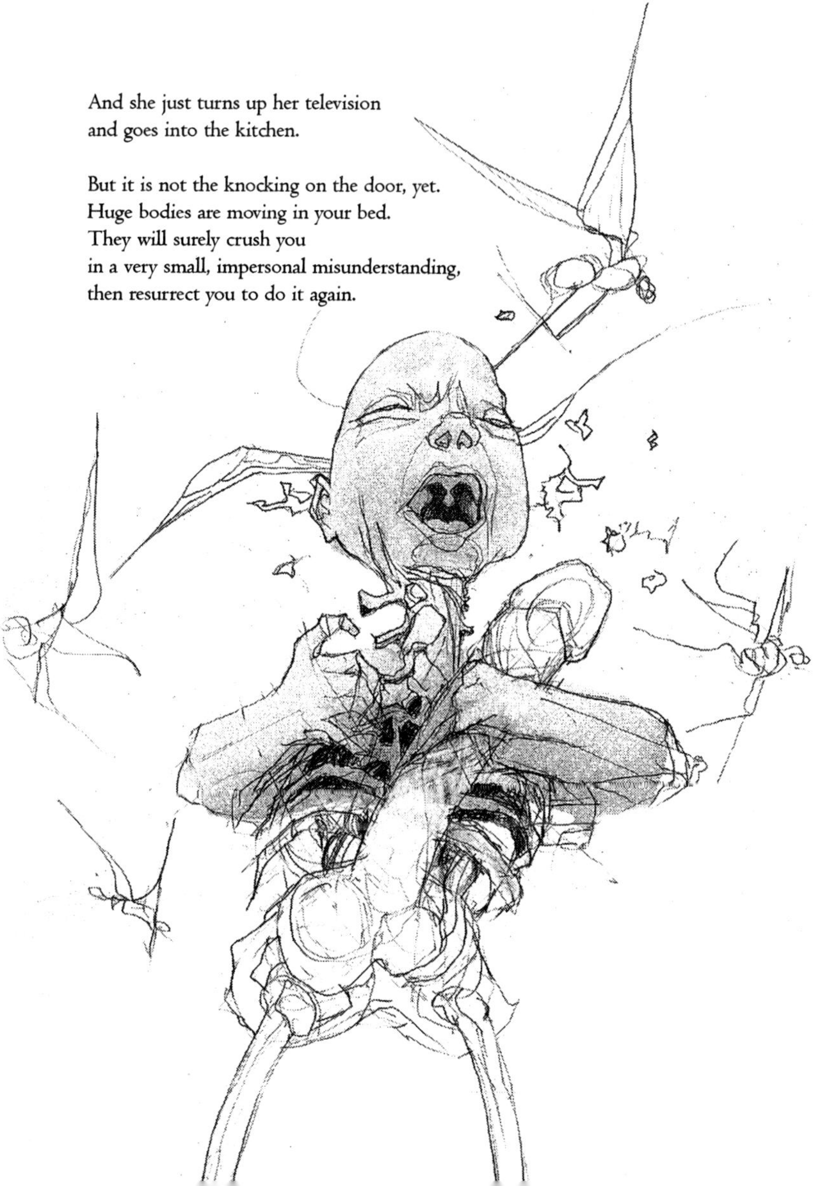

Love Through a Broken Window

My Lover is the one
I can't stop hurting
and the one I can't avoid apologizing to.
My shakti, my shekinah, my consort,
your veil is dark.
The trouble in your look is the failure
and the triumph of our coupling.

The divine sleep has been interrupted.
All the serenity on earth has been shattered.
We are lovers in the lost tribes
of the broken window.
Who are we to expect that we can heal
any of it
with our fervent kisses?

In our truces, each side wonders
if it would have made out better
had it fought a little harder,
held out a little longer.
I tried to walk away.
But the kundalini with its bloody sex teeth
had awakened. I acquiesced. The fight continues.

My feelers are faulty.
I leapt into the breach between me and you
and made things worse.
Pissing into an empty grave,
while bullets whistle by
requires a calm and even mind.
But not as much as beauty does.

All my openings reach for you.
My nerves hunger for nerves nearby.
The usual brutal wisdom seems out of place.
I am waiting in wartime for a return to our senses,
or at least to our desires.
I know us. We hide from each other everywhere.
But we give great hints.

More or Less

I always thought this
would have happened before.
But this is a first.
I'm so much better than anyone.
But lord I'm so much worse.

You keep track of the breaths, of the steps
It takes to get a glass of water,
Like I'm the son from the bad side of the eclipse
And you're heaven's suffering daughter.

It's cold here. But I know that will end.
I need you, if not in my bed, then as a friend.
I know that's a lie.
But if you won't break, please at least bend.

And I got a lot of secrets.
But I want to tell them.
And I got few regrets.
But I want to quell them.

It's the kisses I don't give
That make you love me more.
It's the life I should live
That makes life such a bore.

The sun shone on my shoulders, more or less.
I gave the effort
Everything, but it wouldn't take my best.

So now I'm human, for better and worse.
Part of me's mine and part of me's hers.

My Lover in Wartime

She calls to warn me
about bombs on the subway.
She loves me,
digs her heels in as I careen.

I am too ambivalent
to make anything but a mess
of her love.
She knows this.
We follow each others' lead.

There is a war all around us.
The gods are horny too.
Maybe the old prizes are in play
more than they were yesterday.

Stick It, Conscript

In the trembling fires of adolescence,
the command came down to us,
pronounced by every human face
and every human creation:
"Stick it where it stinks."

Those were hard days,
when we were conscripted
into the armies of sex

and made to live at close quarters
with our half-embarrassed marching orders.

INITIATION

With one ejaculation,
I was exiled from mythology
and pushed onto the streets.
I made my debut in that birth canal
that never gives birth,
but only replaces and replaces.

I found a spastic moment of peace.
And it bothered me more than loneliness did.
Its relief was just one more law sunk into me.
I was no match for that peace.
I spent half my time chasing it down
and the other half trying to escape it.

I wanted my desire to swell enough
to dissolve the rest of me
or to vanish altogether.

Neither occurred.

Thusly Humbled

She asks for emotions I haven't seen in years.
She says she is a prize to be fought for.
The magazines and the tv tell me the same,
saying her favors are worth every fortune.

But one voice, whispering under duress,
says she is only a consequence, a circumstance,
that her body is the engine
of a world I never trusted,
that the desires that murmur all around it
are like gasoline fumes.

But it is too late.
I'm inside that world.
It's an initiation my woman celebrates
with her wild man.
                The initiation is not like rock and roll.
                It's not like anything else at all,
                like all initiations are.

In it, I become something more specific than myself,
something smaller, more common,
better able to fit inside.
                But I like how she smothers me.
                It's scarier than the massive spaces
                I've grown around myself.

"Baby," I say with my hands.
"I am willing to learn all the poisonous things."
She lets me drink of her lethe.

Thusly humbled, I begin to move
to the most obscure part of the world,
the center.

Summer

In the summer,
I learned the strange laws of desire.

How to draw nearer to the one I want
by pulling away.

Delirious, my lover and I rolled
on the floor, drank fruit punch from the chandelier.

It was no longer sex we were engaged in,
but the taking of barnacles from our bloodless bodies,

the shedding of tired nerves
that no longer carried their own weight.

We talked pure nonsense there,
in that gift from our bodies.

The sky was irrelevant,
the city was irrelevant. My gaze fixed on nothing.

By late August, I was too competent a lover
to return to the hermitage.

The Blue Blueprint

You:

Pretend for a minute
that you are the man who is sated
and forgoes the gold
in the farther hill

and that all the hungers
have unraveled to reveal
just hunger

and that you are
not much more
than that.

You still race the food in your stomach
to see who will eat who first.
You win awhile.

THE TOWN:

In the land
of the retired babylionaire,
a frenzy stirs.

Wives remodel kitchens again and again.
Husbands shrug their shoulders
and go to work.

The retired ziggurat of garbage
gets a little lower each year.

They are taking the new garbage
to a spot a little farther
from the shopping plaza.

The town races the food in its stomach
to see who will eat who first.

It wins awhile.

THE DREAM:

The resentment of men
whose lives are guaranteed
and set on old roads
eats those roads.

When the dream
made of streets and traffic signs
finally fouls its own bed,

the only way to keep god out of pornography
is to vehemently prohibit him a visage
and to place him beyond the lascivious imagination.

And if any man is to keep his name in a void
whose only voice is appetite,
then the most invisible, fragile thing
must be kept sated.

It took all of the bad side of egypt
to teach the jews that.

The dream races the men in its stomach
to see who will eat who first.
It wins awhile.

Now:

Now, in lieu of pyramid tops,
a big mortgage looms.
Whoever we are
has bought the future. And we pay big.

There are no more icons,
no more fixed images to look upon.
The world is the place
that gives back everything
tainted and strange.

There is only a triumph, a train of pomp
moving past or moving through,
depending on who you get to be.

Here, in the future's ruins,
we reach out in all directions
for signs of an accomplice
in our mildly doomed scheme.

We are growing corn in the graveyard.
Grandpa's coming back to dinner.
You are nothing but now.

The Blue Blueprint

The Beginning

"What's the matter with before?"
ask the injured angels,
lamenting the new cure.

Yeah, the angels are in play
for us crazed men who say, beneath a cough,
that we caught the gods jacking off.

We giggle out here, far beyond pity.
Although it seems so far from the beginning
that even the ghosts wear masks
as they show us the city.

Show Us the City

They tell me uptown and true north differ,
that life is a garage at the end of a driveway
and the inside of a star is quieter
than the benches by the sinking piers.

They speak from a place
where the myths have cooled
to something as regular
as a mailman's route.

They crowd the center but don't dare enter.
They tell me the city is a dirty aberration

and not a proxy for the hopes of man
or the dreams of the earth.

But I am not innocent.
I drank the finest wine and paid in fraud.
I ate the biggest steak and lied to the waiter.

Once, I took my honest-gotten meat
to the woods, in the cool of autumn.
But the fire-pit filled in with dirt
and a wolf ran off with dinner.

I chased the wolf into the suburbs.
And it dropped the meat in a driveway.
I picked it up and bit in.

But everyone was watching--
the moms getting the mail,
the dads parking their cars,
the kids in the frontyards.

They were the Stars
of the scene.

Off with Dinner

Transcendence is full of objects,
full of weather, I hear.
It's like the imagination of amoebas
and other unrealizable projects.

The front becomes the rear,
an eye becomes a maze,
the straight line sweats rings.
Things that aren't always things
move in and out of phase,
becoming familiar, but never clear.

The transcendence I fled and the one I bought
turned out to be the same.
It is all for naught.
And naught is my middle name.

Transcendence is Full of Objects

If one small thing seems improbable,
it is because you are dreaming.

I remember this rule
over a chicken dinner,
after a day of work,

when I can't recognize
a football team's helmet
on the television.

Because You Are Dreaming

The paint in the motel
peels in small pieces.
Each detail is a lesson, listen.

The secrets hide in shadows, and well,
under misplaced toilet articles,
in the bedsheet's creases.

It is a part of the holy design,
the blue blueprint, which may yet prove benign,
that the secrets are so hidden.

Between breaths,
a mystery is in estrus.

Through the early morning,
the secrets emerge
between dreams, overripe and monstrous.

Only constant ritual will forestall disaster
in the hours I steal.

I hold off the oceans, the stars
and the nightmares cast in alabaster
with a crap, a wash, a breath, a meal,
then another.

It is tedious work, devoid of skill.
But for the privilege of doing it,
almost anyone would kill.

A Mystery in Estrus

The universe opens pornographically
above the beach.
Divided along a line of foam,
the stars and town lights reach.

Mars is bright in the sky, the waves pound.
Toward each step, a million homicides climb.
The world is war, but only playful,
once it's killed you a few times.

The sharks roam like cops in the ocean.
In the television, dinosaurs parade
like new model cars, wearing my emotions.

I'm not out to castrate a planet
or blind the cyclops eye of the sun.
Summer's wish was too well granted.
It oppresses the beach with unrelenting fun.

Playful, Once It's Killed You

I committed my crimes
while I was sleeping.
But they will come
for me all the same.

I will try not to shake.
I will try to learn.

But does anyone ever learn?
Does the wanting ever quiet enough?
The world is addictive,
as all the scared sacred voices warn.

And the addiction
has a way of dissolving warnings
like time dissolves men.

I tried desperately to forge
the heavenly receipt
in every moment I thought I was awake.

But I signed my work while I was sleeping.
And they will come
for me all the same.

THE HEAVENLY RECEIPT

The angel that wrestled jacob for one night
has made a project of me.

He beats me all day.
He is not strong, but unrelenting.

He loses the fight daily
and tells me the holy names nightly.

But he always gets his knocks in and makes me forget
or bitterly recall those names later on.

He changes my name to israel,
then to shithead.

I say uncle. I hide in wishes.
But my brother the angel does not stop.

Then to Shithead

Perfection flees me.
Having no leads, I overturn every rock,
look into every star, indulge every fate
no matter how poisonous.

The zoologists on the tv
are still trying to figure out
what we were up to when we were spiders,
what we longed for and what we left behind us.

Most of all,
the zoologists want to know
how they made life work as spiders
and how they might again.

It's spiders all the way to the smallmost,
tonight.

They hide in molecules,
in strange ancient atoms
that the universe doesn't make anymore.

Step up and sing into the microscope, spidey.
I see your webs,
but you always hide when I come around.

What have I longed for?
What have I left behind?
These questions do not stop.

I answer them and they swallow their answers.
I spin webs, but all I catch is me.

Atoms the Universe Doesn't Make

We are the gypsies

of human incarnation,

always showing up

too few and too late

to be anything more

than a curiosity.

More than a Curiosity

Don't know how nor why nor when.
But somebody painted a picture.
And hung it in the opium den.

But I can't complain too much.
Except about the banging and such.

Too hungry, too horny or too high
To ever notice or wonder why
Someone hung on every whorehouse wall
A picture of anything at all.

On the senate floor, older than the chore,
The girls all sing until they're sore,
While the men disagree on what they're for.

But I can't complain too much.
Except about the banging and such.

A fellow patient tried to tell me why
There were pictures on the walls of the opium den.
But when everyone's so hungry, horny or high,
You can't really trust even a friend.

They can't look me in the eye,
They stare into my mouth when I say hi.

But I wouldn't complain too much
About the pictures on the whorehouse wall.
I still recall where I left my crutch
And the night I made those pictures fall.

Stare into My Mouth

We know where we're from,
where the treasure is buried,
which rock to look under, which star
to look behind, which fate is our own.

But we can not trust ourselves.
It is not diffidence.
We have real reasons not to trust ourselves.

The fiery guilt in our minds
is not for nothing.
We are not built for wisdom.

Our memories and attention spans
suffice only to propel a mystery.

Not Built for Wisdom

I spurned those who wanted
to be closer to me
because you can't be god
in someone else's heaven.

I told myself and them
that I wouldn't be around too long,
that I heard music in my head
that was really music.

Only a sound, a voice
that exists completely
before giving a hint of itself
can appear like that, like music.

And I wouldn't be so
selfish
if it didn't seem that what I had
was so specifically my own.

Someone Else's Heaven

No one would ever explain the loose ends,
the ones who were more or less thwarted young,
the ones who filled the time or killed the time,
the old stories of hungry, bloody flowers,
the staircases with secrets inside,
the angry women carrying bundles of flowers,
the cartoons in the old man's will,
the hunters setting traps for themselves,
the man whose body is a writing instrument,
the granite heart that makes the trains go,
the sadness in the granite heart,
the architect who cannot draw an exit,
the many rituals busily fucking the many fears,
the one good thought
that keeps the sky from crushing the people,
or the ones who took the bet
that starts in pain and ends in debt.

Cartoons in His Will

One mountain over, we're carving a horse.
And though we may, in a matter of course,
for now we won't say why.

But simply put,
it's a portrait of you and I.

Later civilizations
will see the horse and recall the cart
and know what variety of knowledge
we have to impart.

Later Civilization

Good times. The deity leaves big tips.
And I can hear the music in my hips.
I spend these years trying to find
The boiling temperature of wine.

I hunt for luxury, for vacant cheeriness,
But only to pass through it.
As if it would wash away my weariness
In ways I can't intuit.

My highest aim is criminal,

I just don't know what crime.

My trial is subliminal

And takes up most of my time.

All the truths have been plundered,

The covenants been sundered,

The successes been blundered,

The endgames been wondered.

The players chewed the scenery
until there was nothing left to see.

And it's so damn hard to be brave

When even the whores own slaves.

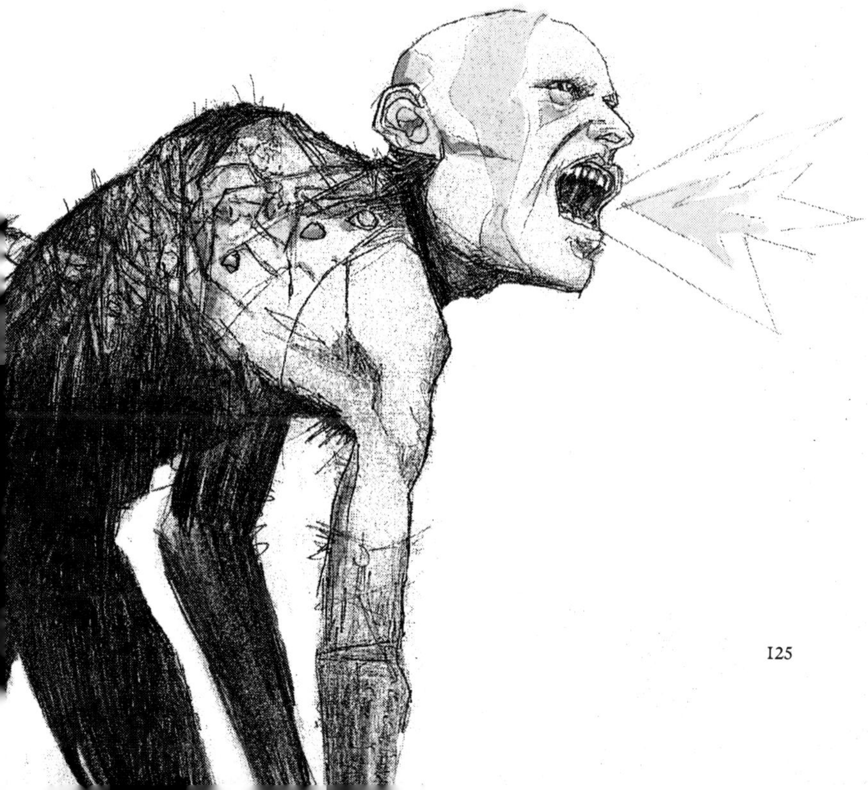

Plundered Truths

I fight every night
with my parents
over painkilling drugs
left over from a recent death.

We are the gods who vastly
misunderstood heaven.
We are working out the kinks
with our broken bones and shabby brains.

Left Over from a Recent Death

The beginning
is always a catastrophe.
Your mother
must turn terrifying
for you to leave home.

Not Infinite

1. A Hell of a Riddle

The body is the problem
dividing the cosmos from itself.
It is an unpaid-for land with unheard-of customs--
a hell of a riddle.

Unpaid-for, unheard-of.
A feeling of strangeness and shame
swaddles tomorrow as it swaddles today.

Wild new hungers wait over the hill
for something no one can yet say.
We'll call it a woman for now.

She is a fantastic forgotten thing,
who escapes still,
like Atlantis sinking deeper into the ocean floor,
under the burden of her own guilt.

2. The Grand Project

The patterns
that were melted out of Aztec gold
reassert themselves in contrails
across the afternoon sky
and in the woodwork of small-town bars,
where disreputable families
while away the generations.

They build houses
that keep out the cold
and you hear no more from them.
Their world rests in the cheap omniscience
of finite desires and imaginations.
Their troubles have been lulled to sleep.

Even their sleep has been lulled to sleep.
But the earth will not digest
all of the bottles they leave in the yard.
Searchers from later ages--dirt in their fingernails
and a jigsaw gleam in their eyes--will come.

And against their will,
they will uncover only
themselves, large and small
and inescapable.

3. Chewing Gum

Everyone here chews gum.
It is the fucking we need
without the grand finale.

The wind of the addict and the prophet
blows toward the grand finale.
The dog-faced houses guard against the wind.

We householders want
the holy unspeakable name sung out
by a voice like a criminal gunshot.

We want the assassination
of time before and time after,
to release us from the debts we owe to each.

We want it enough to fear it more than anything
in our moment of stasis, when the sun is pale
and filtered through curtains.

In the houses, the grand project
slowly works into its true form,
which is the opposite of a culmination.

Time in those wooden brains
is as thick as chewed gum
and barely passes.

4. Civilization in My Gut

The first voice gets me up to date.
I haven't been playing the radio.
There's war on the airwaves,
and chickenwings in my gut.

Life goes on. Civilizations
rise and fall in my body
in time with the day's mix
of drugs and cooked meats.

My nights are quiet. I hear them all:
The civilizations that worship the great mother,
that yearn and grope toward the first birth,
that die by the sword, the law and the facts of science,
that pass over uninherited plains meeting no one,
that know the dramas of the stars as they know their own,
that fuck and kill and think nothing of it
but think of nothing else.

Each one takes root in my body,
reaches ripeness and rots
from boredom, incest, apathy,
leaves traces, but leaves just the same.

5. The Story

The story shines

through my artifact

of a body.

It interrupts itself

to start over

with each new eye that opens.

In the story, thousands die badly

to make a single point,

to teach each simple lesson.

If there is a system to it,

if there is a wisdom to it,

it is a messy system, a messy wisdom.

The story is more than free.

I have to pay and pay

to hear anything else.

6. The Pride of Being

The Pride of Being,
the inverse of the Bewilderment of Birth,
propels the story,
compels the cascading generations.

It forces the issue,
directs men and women to fight
the protracted war
versus nothinghood.

The Pride of Being
is the standard and the one
who carries the standard
before a bewildered army.

7. Creation and Its Weariness

What kind of creatures are we?
    Cigarette smoke hisses
    into the windowless bathroom.
    It is saturday night,
    time to answer
    that question again.

    I will tell our story, the one
about creation and its weariness of itself.
    This time, I'll tell it in the form
    of a love affair with the woman
    in the black blouse and short skirt
    sitting under the tv.

    She lights a cigarette.
    She's looking at me
    out of the whites of her eyes,
    out of her cigarette.
    She seems concerned about the thing
    directly above me, behind me.

8. The Message, the Command

It is too late to forget.
The memory is too strong.
I am a limb in its body.

My autonomy is only
the memory's fevered bid
to escape from itself.

But it is not time to remember.
The present story is too intimate,
its next curve is too arousing.

Meanwhile, the story unfolds slowly, telling
of every failed escape from our inescapable selves.
And I feel it. And it is real.

The memory tells it all instantaneously,
if you aren't careful. But there is no lesson in it,
except one too extreme to be useful.

The memory's message is forever garbled.
It urges the recipient to both get on with the story
and to get to the point.

9. Like in Dante

The world is not infinite,
I am just particularly finite.
Getting born was as close to escape as I got.

There is a parking lot, a hill,
and beyond that, there's a hill
and another parking lot, still.

With the threat of nothinghood gaping,
We fuck and interrupt each other's fucking,
never quite leaving nor quite returning.

We damned, like in Dante, swirl.
But we call it a night out.

The gum-chewing angel
brandishes a flaming sword.
at the threshold of the world.

And he pitches the grand project
to whoever can't avoid overhearing him

And I conduct all of the night's dirty, secret business
only to dive so deeply into the world
that I can stop seeing him.

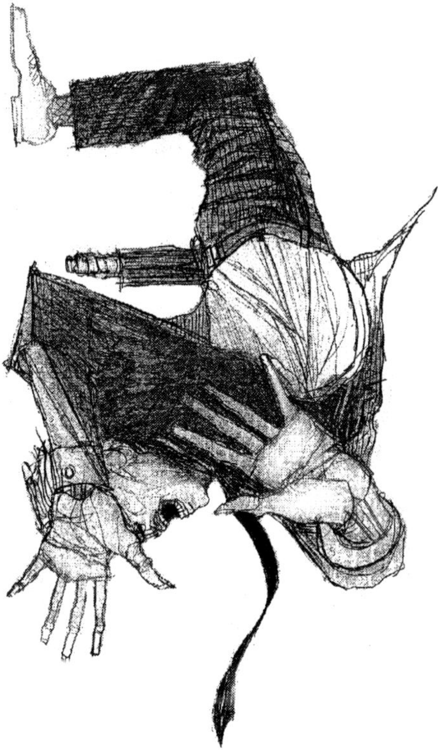

Colin Dodds was born in the twentieth century. He grew up in Central Massachusetts. After a brief, disastrous stint out West,, he completed his formal education in New York City. He currently works as a journalist and lives in Brooklyn, New York, by the river. His poems have appeared in *The Wall Street Journal Online, Folio, Copious Magazine, Main Street Rag, Sidereality, Jack Magazine* and *The Gallatin Review*. His first book of poems, *The Last Man on the Moon* (Medium Rare Publishing) came out in 2002. And more books are on their way.

Ben Gibson graduated from Parsons School of Design in the late nineteen-nineties. He is an illustrator and graphic designer and lives in New York City. He stands six feet tall and weighs in at two hundred eighty pounds, though he lies about his weight. A former high-school pitcher with a solid curveball, he often wonders what might have been, and drinks. Otherwise his past is a blur to both himself and others. His codename is "The Lone Falcon." In addition to *The Blue Blueprint*, he also designed the album cover of the rock-and-roll version of *The Last Man on the Moon* for Medium Rare Records. Ben's favorite movie is *Care Bears 3, The Reckoning*. He is a mischievous boy and he hates you a lot.

Dan Jock graduated from Parsons School of Design in 1997. He plans to draw until he can no longer see. Dan has seen action doing graphics for some of the premier institutions in the land. Prior to a short stint in aerospace (government-classified), he was fired from Nickelodeon in 1998 for riding a child's bicycle without permission. Shortly afterward, he was waived by Kinko's for insulting a corporate trainer by farting. Dan now rides in limousines for a living in Santa Barbara, California.

ALSO, BE SURE TO CHECK OUT THESE OTHER GREAT TITLES AVAILABLE EXCLUSIVELY FROM MEDIUM RARE PUBLISHING!

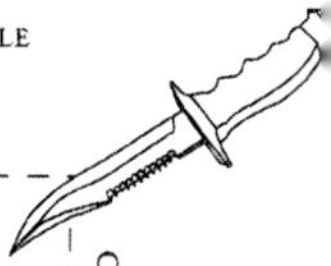

THE LAST MAN ON THE MOON Colin Dodds	THE LAST MAN ON THE MOON, THE ORIGINAL CAST RECORDING Matt Dublin and Colin Dodds	PIG'S BIG WIN Peter Clime
THE CHRISTMAS HALL OF FAME Dan Jock	THE SMARTASS AND THE DUMBASS Joe Martin	WISDOM'S REAL OPPOSITE OR 101 POEMS ABOUT AN ODYSSEY ON A STOOL Calvin Dodge
BROWN SUGAR, WHY DO YOU TASTE SO GOOD? Benjamin Gibson	HIGH ROLLING IN THE WEIMAR REPUBLIC Will Wheaton	SOME KIND OF RECORD Calvin Dodge
ICE CREAM ALL DAY Joseph Jock	HEAVE'S END- THE GREAT DAY Colin Dodds	KEN GIBSON AND THE CASE OF THE LONE FALCON Benjamin Gibson

Cut Along the Dotted Line

For a complete catalogue of all Medium Rare Publishing books
and Medium Rare Records CDs, send $3.50 to:
Medium Rare Industries, Brooklyn Branch
65 South 6th St.
Brooklyn, NY 11211
or visit us at: www.mediumrarepub.com